David Vance

Narrative of the Battle of Cowan's Ford, February 1st, 1781

David Vance

Narrative of the Battle of Cowan's Ford, February 1st, 1781

ISBN/EAN: 9783337182335

Printed in Europe, USA, Canada, Australia, Japan

Cover: Foto ©ninafisch / pixelio.de

More available books at **www.hansebooks.com**

NARRATIVE

OF THE

BATTLE OF COWAN'S FORD,

FEBRUARY 1ST, 1781,

BY ROBERT HENRY,

AND

Narrative of the Battle of Kings Mountain,

BY CAPTAIN DAVID VANCE.

———

MANUSCRIPT PRESERVED BY ROBERT HENRY, ESQ.

———

COPY FURNISHED BY LYMAN C. DRAPER, LL. D.,

OF MADISON, WISCONSIN.

———

PUBLISHED BY D. SCHENCK, SR.

Greensboro, N. C., March 28th, 1891.

———

Reece & Elam, Printers.

PREFACE.

Having seen the following most valuable and interesting narrative quoted very often in "KING'S MOUNTAIN AND ITS HEROES," written by Lyman C. Draper, L. L. D., of Wisconsin, I wrote the Doctor with a view of obtaining the original manuscript if possible, but was unable to procure it. He however very generously intrusted to me the following copy which he had himself "carefully transcribed" from the original paper in his hands, in January 1874, and which had been sent to him by Dr. J. F. E. Hardy, of Asheville, North Carolina. The original manuscript had been placed in Dr. Hardy's possession by Wm. L. Henry, of Buncombe County, a son of Robert Henry— William L. Henry is still living.

In a note to "King's Mountain and its Heroes," page 259, is the following brief sketch of Robert Henry, who was wise enough to preserve this contribution to our Revolutionary history—to-wit:

"Mr. Henry was born in a rail pen, in then Rowan,* now Iredell county, North Carolina, January 10th 1765. Full of patriotism though young, he shared in the trials and perils of the Revolution, and in due time recovered from the severe wounds he received at King's Mountain. In 1795, he was one of the party who ran the boundary line between North Carolina and Tennessee. He subsequently studied law, and practiced his profession many years in Buncombe County. He served in the House of Commons in 1833 and 1834. He was a clear and forcible public speaker; and his memory deserves to be held in grateful remembrance for preserving the narrative of the

*This is manifestly an error. He was born in Tryon. See W. L. Henry's letter to Dr. Hardy. Tryon was changed to Lincoln County. Lincoln was divided and Mr. Henry's birthplace is in the present Gaston county.

King's Mountain campaign and battle, so frequently cited in this work. He died in the new County of Clay, North Carolina, January 6th, 1863, within four days of attaining the patriarchal age of ninety-eight years, and he was undoubtedly the last of the heroes of King's Mountain."

Robert Henry lived in the vicinity of Tuckaseage Ford, on the Catawba river, which is about ten miles below Cowan's Ford, when Cornwallis crossed at the latter ford. He lived on the West side of the river in Lincoln County. For many years he owned the White Sulphur Springs about five miles South west of Asheville. It was a popular resort in the summer for the wealthy planters from the South and was the scene of much gayety and pleasure. Mr. Henry died in Clay County, the extreme Western county of the State, bordering on Georgia and Tennessee. I have myself heard my grandfather Michael Schenck, of Lincolnton, N. C., speak of Mr. Henry as "a great land lawyer." His practice as a surveyor, no doubt, making him formidable in such suits.

The public is indebted to the Hon. Theodore F. Davidson, Attorney General of North Carolina, and a great-grandson of Captain David Vance, for the publication of this narrative.

D. SCHENCK, Senior.

Greensboro, N. C., March the 28th, 1891.

ROBERT HENRY'S NARRATIVE.

KING'S MOUNTAIN BATTLE, &c.

To Dr. J. F. E. Hardy,
      Asheville, N. C.:

My Dear Sir, and Kind Friend:

    I send you the MS. of my father, Robert Henry. He was born in Tryon (now Lincoln) county, N. C., *in a rail pen,* 10th February, 1765; was a lawyer and surveyor by profession; was one of the first settlers in Buncombe county; taught School on Swannanoa, the first school taught in Buncombe county. He died in Clay county, N. C., February 6th, 1863, wanting but four days of being 98 years old. Thomas Henry, his father, died soon after the Revolution, of rheumatism contracted during the war. Thomas Henry was from the North of Ireland.

    I do not want this manuscript lost, as you see it is in Robert Henry's own hand, and a little relic. If not used, I should like it should be returned to

                    Respectfully,
                    WM. L. HENRY,
                        Asheville,
              Buncombe County, N. C.

ROBERT HENRY'S NARRATIVE.

I will proceed to point out and correct some of the errors in WHEELER'S HISTORY of North Carolina, so far as respects the transactions of Cornwallis crossing Cowan's Ford, on Catawba river, the 1st of February, 1781; then I will give my own version of that transaction; then I will give the common report of the transaction shortly after it happened.

Wheeler's History, p. 232-'33: "Here" (meaning at Cowan's Ford) "about six hundred militia under General Davidson were posted, and a slight skirmish occurred. A British Colonel (Hall) and three privates were killed, and thirty-six wounded."

If we take this account to be true, we must conclude that these militia were very bad marksmen, for they had time to have fired five rounds each, which would have been three thousand single shots, at distances varying from fifty yards to less than twenty yards, over a naked sheet of water; that their enemy was not obscured by smoke, being in water above the waist-band, and hanging together by their muskets; that not a single gun was fired by them whilst in the water. This story, if it bears telling, cannot be accredited to be true, that in firing three thousand single shots they only killed four, including Col. Hall, and wounded thirty-six. The story appears further incredible from this—that in common battles on land, there are as many, and often more, men killed than wounded where the whole force from head to foot is exposed to fire of the opposite party. In the present case, the body, from above the waist-band to the top of the head was exposed—for all below was under water and secure from lead. Wounds in the upper part [of the body] are doubly as apt to kill as those in the lower extremities, from the waist-band downward; hence we would expect double as many killed on this occasion as wounded—but the reverse is told, that only four were killed, including Col. Hall, and thirty-six wounded.

A further mistake may be noticed. The account states that Davidson had six hundred militia, whereas he had only three hundred. The whole of this quotation should pass for nothing.

The next error that I will notice is on page 235 of Wheeler's History, which I quote: "Soon after the action commenced" (meaning at Cowan's Ford) "General William Davidson was killed, greatly lamented by all who knew him as a talented, brave and generous officer." The true statement is this: Davidson was killed by the first gun that was fired on the British side on that occasion, for they did not fire a gun whilst in the river; and the gun that killed him was fired at the water's edge on the Mecklenburg side; and if Davidson's clothes had been examined, it is probable that they would have shown the mark of powder. The whole of the Americans had left their stands or posts at the water's edge and judiciously fle l, lest the British might hem them in by the river; and an utter silence prevailed—not a gun firing on either side: Silence was first broken by the report of the gun that killed Davidson.

A further quotation from the same page: "The Company commanded by Gen. Graham was the first to commence the attack" (at Cowan's Ford) "on the British as they advanced through the river, which was resolutely continued until they reached the bank, loaded their arms, and commenced a heavy fire upon his men, two of whom were killed." The whole of this is a gratuitous statement, for Gen. Graham was not there—nor was there either officer or private killed at that place except Gen. Davidson ; nor was there any one wounded there except Robert Beatty, who afterwards died of the wound. Gen.

Graham and his company may have been at Davidson's camp, three quarters of a mile from the Ford, and two of his men might have been killed there, if they were too tardy in making their escape before the British arrived there.

Another quotation from Wheeler's History, p. 264: " At day break the British army under Cornwallis, on the 1st February, 1781, entered the waters of Catawba, then swollen by heavy rains, at Cowan's Ford. The morning was dark and rainy. The light infantry under Col. Hall entered first, followed by the grenadiers and the battalions. The piquet of Gen. Davidson challenged the enemy; receiving no reply the guard fired. This turned out the whole force of Davidson, who kept up a galling fire from the bank."

Observe the morning was dark but not rainy. Davidson's army was stationed three quarters of a mile from the Ford, and did not fire a gun at the British whilst in the river, nor after they came across; all the firing by the American side in the river and on the bank was done by the guard.

Now, I will give my own version of the transaction of Cornwallis crossing Catawba River at Cowan's Ford, 1st February, 1781. Robert Beatty, a lame man, had taken up a school near the Tuckaseage Ford, and had taught two days, and was teaching the third, when news came to the School-house that Cornwallis was camped at Forney's, about seven miles from the School-house; that Tarleton was ranging through the country catching whig boys to make musicians of them in the British army. The master instantly dismissed the scholars, directing them to go home and spread the news, and retired himself. I went home, and that night Moses Starret, Alexander Starret, George Gillespie, Robert Gillespie, and Charles Rutledge came to my father's! We lay out that night, and shortly before day-light my brother, Joseph Henry, who had left the army to give the news, and had crossed Catawba at John Beattie's in a canoe; and when he left the army, it was expected that Cornwallis would cross the river at Tuckaseage Ford. Early in the morning this company crossed the river at Beatties, about two miles below Tuckoseage Ford, where we hid our canoe, staid some time at Beatties'—then went up to the Tuckaseage Ford, and the army was at Cowan's Ford, we went up the river to John Nighten's, who treated us well by giving us potatoes to roast, and some whisky to drink. We became noisy and mischievous. Nighten said we should not have any more whisky. I proposed to go to the camp at the Ford, if any one would let me have a gun and ammunition. My brother said he would give me his; Charles Rutledge proposed also to accompany me if he had a gun and ammunition; when Moses Starret gave him his gun. When about to start, I gave Nighten a hundred dollar Continental bill for a half a pint of whisky. My brother gave another bill of the same size for half a bushel of potatoes. We dispatched the whiskey, Being thus equipped, we went to the Ford, which was about a mile and a half. When we arrived, the guard that was there, thirty in number, made us welcome; the officer of the guard told us that Cornwallis would certainly attempt to cross that night or early in the morning; that each one of the guard had picked their stands to annoy the British as they crossed, so that when the alarm was given they would not be crowded, or be in each other's way—and said we must choose our stands. He accompanied us—Charles Rutledge chose the uppermost stand, and I chose the lowest, next the getting out place of the Ford; the officer observed, that he considered that Davidson had done wrong, for that the army should have been stationed at the Ford—instead of

which it was encamped three-fourths of a mile off, and
that some person acquainted in the neighborhood of
Forney should watch the movements of Cornwallis' army,
and immediately when they would attempt to march, to
to hasten to the river and give the alarm; then that Davidson's army might be in readiness to receive them; the
river being in the situation that it was then in, and the
army thus prepared to receive them, said that Cornwallis
and a million of men coul 1 not cross without can-
non as long as our ammunition would last. This I
thought was a large expression; but since I think he was
correct.* He mentioned to each man of the guard to go
to his stand again and examine it, so that when the
alarm was given, that there should be no mistakes then
made. I went to mine, and was well pleased with it—
for in shooting, if I would miss my first aim, my lead
would range along the British army obliquely and still
do damage, and that I could stand it until the British
would come to a place the water was riffling over a rock,
then it would be time to run away. I remember that I
looked over the guard to see if there was any person with
whom I was acquainted, and found none but Joel Jetton,
and my lame school-master, Robert Beatty, with my
comrade, Charles Rutledge.

Gen. Joseph Graham's name is mentioned by Wheeler.
I was acquainted with him; but he was not there. Shortly after dark a man across the river hooted like an owl,
and was answered; a man went to a canoe some distance
off, and brought word from him that all was silent in the
British camp. The guard all lay down with their guns
in their arms, and all were sound asleep at day-break,
except Joel Jetton, who discovered the noise of horses in
deep water. The British pilot, Dick Beal being deceived

---

*Gen. Greene had admonished Davidson of the danger of Tarleton crossing secret-
ly at some private ford and falling on his rear, and for this reason he kept his main
force at some distance from the river.   D. S.

by our fires, had led them into swimming water. Jetton
ran to the Ford, the sentry being sound asleep, Jetton
kicked him into the river, endeavored to fire his gun, but
it was wet: Having discovered the army, ran to our fires,
having a fine voice, cried "the British! the British!" and
fired a gun—then each man ran to his stand; when I got
to my stand, I saw them red, but thought from loss of
sleep my eyes might be mistaken, threw water into them;
by the the time I was ready to fire, the rest of the guard
had fired. I then heard the British splashing and making
a noise as if drowning. I fired, and continued firing until
I saw that one on horse-back had passed my rock in the
river, and saw that it was Dick Beal moving his gun
from his shoulder, I expected, to shoot me. I ran with
all speed up the bank, and when at the top of it, William
Polk's horse breasted me, and Gen. Davidson's horse,
about twenty or thirty feet before Polk's horse, and near
to the water's edge. All being silent on both sides, I
heard the report of a gun, at the water's edge, being the
first gun fired on the British side, and which I thought
Dick Beal had fired at me. That moment Polk wheeled
his horse, and cried "fire away, boys; there is help at
hand." Turning my eye round, designing to run away,
I saw my lame school-master, Beatty, loading his gun by
a tree; I thought I could stand it as long as he could,
and commenced loading. Beatty fired, then I fired, the
heads and shoulders of the British being just above the
bank; they made no return fire; silence still prevailed.
I observed Beatty loading again; I ran down another
load—when he fired, he cried "it's time to run, Bob." I
looked past my tree, and saw their guns lowered, and
then staightened myself behind my tree. They fired and
knocked off some bark from my tree.

In the meantime Beatty had turned from his tree, and
a bullet hit him in the hip, and broke the upper end of his

thigh bone; he fell, still hallowing for me to run. I then ran at the top of my speed about one hundred yards, when a thought struck me that the British had no horsemen to follow me, and that Davidson's army would be down at the river, and a battle would take place. Whereupon I loaded my gun, and went opposite to the Ford, and chose a large tree, sat down by it, and fired about fifty yards at the British. They fired several guns toward the place where I was; but their lead did not come nearer to me than about two rods.

I will now account for the great difference between the number of the British killed and those wounded, as stated by Wheeler. The water at the Ford was fully waist-band deep, and in many places much deeper, with a very heavy pressing current, and when a man was killed or badly wounded, the current immediately floated him away, so that none of them that were killed or badly wounded were ever brought to the shore; and none but those slightly wounded reached the bank; Col. Hall fell at the bank--I account for the three British that were killed as stated by Wheeler, in this way: Beatty, the lame schoolmaster, an excellent marksman, fired twice, at a distance of not more than twenty yards, at the British, after they had ascended the high bank, as before stated; and I fired twice about the same distance. I therefore think Beatty being the best marksman killed two, and I killed one.

Wheeler states that on the American side there were two killed: I observe, if there was any one killed that it was not at the river, for the British did not fire a gun whilst in the river, and when they arose the high bank, all were gone but Beatty and myself; that if any were killed, it was at Davidson's camp, three quarters of a mile from the Ford of the river. But I never heard of any one either killed or wounded of the Americans except Robert Beatty on that occasion.

I will give an account of the balance of my route after firing the last time, as heretofore stated. I went down the river to John Beattie's, where we had left our canoe; there I found my company, the two Starrets, the two Gillespies, my brother Joseph, and my comrade Charles Rutledge. I returned the gun to my brother after counting the cartridges—found seven missing—therefore I had fired seven times, as I supposed. The company remained at Beattie's until the next morning; when we took our canoe to cross the river to the Lincoln side, it was proposed that we would go to James Cunningham's fish-trap, and see if there were any fish in it. When we arrived at the trap, there were fourteen dead men lodged in it, several of whom appeared to have no wound, but had drowned. We pushed them into the water, they floated off, and went each to his own home. This is my version of that transaction.

Now, I will give the common report of it. I will begin with the report of Nicholas Gosnell, one of our neighbors, a Tory, who was in Cornwallis' army when they crossed the Catawba at Cowan's Ford. It was frequently repeated from the extraordinary language he used, and from his manner of expression—it is therefore better imprinted on my memory. I will endeavor to give it in his own language: " His Lordship chose Dick Beal for his pilot, as he well know'd the Ford, and a durned pretty pilot he was, for he suffered himself to be led astray by the Rebel fires, and then had to go down to the Ford afterwards; but if he did bad one way, he did good another, for he killed their damned Rebel General. The Rebels were posted at the water's edge—there wan't many on 'em; but I'll be durned if they didn't slap the wad to his Majesty's men suicidally! for a while; for I

saw 'em hollerin and a snortin and a drownin—the river
was full on 'em a snortin, a hollerin and a drownin until
his Lordship reached the off bank; then the Rebels
made straight shirt tales, and all was silent—then I tell
you his Lordship was Bo sure Super gille cristilum [?],*
and when he rose the bank he was the best dog in the
hunt, and not a rebel to be seen." This is the Tory version of Cornwallis crossing Catawba at Cowan's Ford.

The following is the report of every person who lived at
or near the river between Cowan's Ford and Tuckaseage Ford: That a great number of British dead were
found on Thompson's fish-dam, and in his trap, and numbers lodged on brush, and drifted to the banks: that the
river stunk with dead carcases; that the British could not
have lost less than one hundred men on that occasion.

Report of soldiers who were in Davidson's army.
When Wm. Polk returned from the river after General
Davidson was killed at Cowan's Ford, three quarters of
a mile from the Ford—they stated that when William
Polk returned from the Ford, and reported the death of
Gen. Davidson, that some of the army had left, and the
rest were in confusion; that Polk prudently marched
them off, not being able to fight Cornwallis on equal
terms.

*This seems to be some silly slang of that day.

KING'S MOUNTAIN EXPEDITION.

I will now give the statement of Col. D. Vance and Gen. Joseph McDowell of the manner of raising the army to oppose Col. Ferguson—its march—and the defeat of Ferguson.

This part is the statement of Col. Vance; and on a sarcastic and sneering reply by M. Matthews saying that they, to wit the army under Campbell, was a firece and formidable set of chickens, and could make great havoc among eggs, if each one was provided with a stick. This elicited a more extensive reply and statement of the whole affair and its consequences from Gen. J. McDowell. I will first give the reasons why Vance and McDowell made these statements.

The General Assembly of North Carolina made an agreement with that of Tennessee to run and mark the Division line between the two States, and in the year 1799, the State of North Carolina appointed Gen. J. McDowell, Col. David Vance,* and Mussentine Matthews,† commissioners on the part of North Carolina, who associated John Strother and Robert Henry surveyors, with the necessary numbers of chain-bearers, markers, and packhorsemen for that business, who met and went to the White-Top Mountain, a spur of the Stone Mountain, where the Virginia line crossed the latter. Strother did not appear at the commencement. The company were asking a great many detached questions relative to Ferguson's defeat—at length requested that McDowell or Vance would give them a connected account of the whole transaction from first to last. It was agreed that Col. Vance should give that account. The Colonel agreed to do so on consulting with McDowell, our pilot, Gideon

* Member of the House of Commons from Burke, 1791.
† Member of House Commons from Iredell from 1789 to 1802.

Lewis, who had been a news-carrier, and myself, [and relate it] on the first wet day that should happen so that we could not progress with the line.

Accordingly a wet day happened, when we were at the head of the Round-About on the Stone Mountain. Our bark camp was soon fixed, and Col. Vance gave the account, ending with the details of the battle of King's Mountain. Whereupon M. Matthews observed that we (meaning the army) were a fierce and formidable set of blue hen's chickens among eggs, if each one was provided with a stick." This brought a reply from McDowell. That being done, I was provided with a note-book, separate from my surveyor's book, to take down a memorandum of particular things that happened, and commenced taking a memorandum of Vance's account of that transaction. Whereupon Col. Vance, who was an elegant clerk, told me as there was only one surveyor, that I had not time to do it—and if I would give him my book, that he would write it for me, as he had leisure. He took the book, and returned it to me, saying he had paper of his own, at a Spring by the side of Bright's Path in the Bald Ground on the Yellow Mountain. Having taken down his own recollections, and also Gen. McDowell's reply to M. Matthews—which is as follows:

"As I have in some measure to depend on my memory, I will begin with Col. Shelby's retreat after his defeating the British at Ennoree. Col. Charles McDowell had detached Shelby, Sevier, &c., with a party to go round where Ferguson was camped—who defeated the British and Tories at Ennoree. When Col. McDowell received intelligence of Gate's defeat, and sent an express to Col. Shelby to retreat, Gen. Joseph McDowell was then Major, and I was Captain. Col. Shelby called a council of all his officers to know what was best to do. It was agreed that we must make a wood's trip to get round Ferguson and join Col. C. McDowell, carrying the prisoners alternately on horseback, and running on foot short distances. After going some distance, found that Col. C. McDowell had left his camp, and was retreating towards Gilbert Town, we altered our course and overtook him and the main army.

After joining Col. C. McDowell, it was proposed by Cols. Shelby and Sevier that they thought an army of volunteers could be raised to defeat Ferguson, stating that Ferguson's main business was to kill the Whig stock; that he would be at the heads of Broad River, and then go to the head of Catawba to execute that purpose, which would give time to raise an army of volunteers over the mountains, and in Wilkes and Surry counties. All the officers, and some of the privates were consulted, and all agreed that it was right to make the trial to raise an army. It was then agreed that the prisoners should be sent to Virginia; that Cols. Shelby and Sevier and their men should immediately go over the Mountains home and procure volunteers; that Col. Chas. McDowell should send an express to Cols. Cleveland and Herndon in Wilkes for them to raise volunteers; and that Col. C. McDowell should provide some way to preserve the Whig stock on the head of Catawba, and provide some way also to give intelligence of Ferguson's movements.

The prisoners were accordingly dispatched to Virginia. Cols. Shelby and Sevier went immediately over the mountains; and Col. C. McDowell wrote to Cols. Cleveland and Herndon to raise volunteers to be ready to march upon the shortest notice;—he then called the men on the head of Catawba, and first proposed that they who could not go over the mountains, should take protection on the advance of Ferguson and thereby save the whig stock: Daniel Smith (afterwards Colonel),

Thomas Lytle, Robert Patton and J. McDowell of the Pleasant Garden, absolutely refused, and stated that they would drive the Whig stock into the deep coves under the cave of the Black Mountain; that others might take protection and save the stock that remained behind. John Carson, afterwards Colonel, Wm. Davidson, Ben. Davidson and others were appointed to take protection to save the remaining whig stock.

James Jack and Archibald Nail were appointed to be news-bearers over the Yellow Mountains to Shelby and were to be passing continually—that they were to receive the news in the Turkey Cove relative to Ferguson's movements. That Joseph Dobson and James McKoy were to be bearers of the like news to Cols. Cleveland and Herndon, and that they were to receive their news at the Montgomery place, afterwards Joseph Dobson's place.

Col. Ben. Cleveland appointed his brother, Robert Cleveland and Gideon Lewis, our pilot, to be news-bearers from B. Cleveland to Shelby. Thus the news went the rounds as fast as horses could carry their riders.

After Col. C. McDowell had thus arranged his business, he received the news that Ferguson was at Gilbert Town. He then collected all the men that he could procure from Burke county and went to Shelby and Sevier, who had engaged Col. Campbell, of Virginia, also to raise volunteers. The orders given to the volunteers were to equip themselves as quick as possible and have nothing to provide when they were called on to march, but to saddle their horses and march on the shortest notice. Those who could not go supplied those who could with anything they stood in need of. It was also announced to the volunteers by the officers, that a battle with Ferguson was determined upon, and that they might rely on a battle before they returned home.

The news went the rounds by the news-carriers already mentioned, of every thing that happened in Ferguson's camp—until the news came that John Carson had played a supple trick on Ferguson—that having saved almost all the whig stock that had not been driven into the coves by Daniel Smith and company—that Ferguson began to suspect Carson for saving whig stock —there being a large quantity of Tory cattle ranging about the large cane-breaks where David Greenlee lives, and that a party of Ferguson's were fitted out to kill whig stock, and that they designing to go to that place, and another party was going to the Montgomery place— that is the place where Joseph Dobson lives on—for the like purpose. Carson went with the party going to the Montgomery place, without informing the party going to the Greenlee place that the cattle ranging there were Tory stock, the owners being in Ferguson's camp. The parties each went to their places of destination, and re-turned into camp; those who went to the Greenlee place reported that they had killed over one hundred head of three, four, five and six year old rebel steers at the Mc-Gonaugh place. J. Carson observed that he expected that those steers were the stock of Joseph Brown, Dement and Johnstone, who were there in the camp. Whereupon Brown, Dement and Johnstone went and discovered that the steers there killed were every one theirs. This turn-ed the Tories rather against Ferguson; whereupon Fer-guson stated that the Rebels had out-witted him, and that he could not effect his purpose there—that he would start back to Gilbert Town on a given day.

The news was on its passage to Shelby and Cleveland as soon as the breath left Ferguson's mouth—it did not stop day or night—it was soon at the place of destina-tion. Immediately Shelby directed Campbell and his men to meet him at a given time at Wautaga and Sevier

to meet him and Campbell at ten o'clock on a given day
at the Spring in the Bald Ground, on the Yellow Mountain, at the side of Bright's path—all of which were done
with great exactness. He issued orders for Cleveland
and Herndon to meet him on a given day on Silver
Creek, in Burke county; and ordered D. Smith, J. Mc-
Dowell, Lytle, Patton, and those who had taken protection, to meet him at Wm. Nail's by a given night, which
was the night next after the meeting on the Yellow
Mountain.

When the officers met at the Spring on the Yellow
Mountain, it was quickly agreed that they would send
Col. Charles McDowell with an express to Gen. Gates,
for him to send an experienced officer to conduct them
in a battle with Ferguson, and as soon as Chas. Mc-
Dowell, with his silver-mounted Tom. Simpson rifle, had
disappeared, steering for the path on the Linville Ridge,
the army descended the Mountain on Bright's path and
went to Wm. Nail's that night where they met Daniel
Smith, Thomas Lytle, Joseph McDowell and Robert
Patton, the persons who had driven the whig stock into
the coves under the cave of the Black Mountains, and
also those who had taken protection. When it was
agreed, that D. Smith, T. Lytle and J. McDowell should
remain at the head of the river, as they were considered
equal to a small army against Indians; and that the Indians were expected to fall on the frontiers as soon as
Ferguson left it; and that they should have those who
had taken protection to assist them. It was agreed that
Joseph McDowell, (now Gen.) should take twenty men
with him, and follow Ferguson's trail for fear of surprise
—who at the head of Silver Creek, near the Pilot Mountain, came on a squad of Tories who were designing to
follow Ferguson, and killed some of them and put the

rest to flight and returned to the army in the morning after staying the night at Wm. Nails's.

The army marched in to Silver Creek, and at the place appointed met Cols. Cleveland and Herndon so exactly that it scarcely occasioned a halt—proceeding on to Cane Creek of Broad River at a place afterwards called Probit's place.

Major Billy Chronicle with twenty men joined the army; no halt called—still proceeding on. At Camp Creek Cols. William Graham, with one hundred and sixty men well mounted, joined—who gave intelligence that Ferguson had left Gilbert Town and had crossed Broad River at Twitty's Ford on his way to Cruger at Ninety-Six and that Col. Willams was near to Gilbert Town. It was agreed among the officer's [while] still on the march, that Col. Herndon's foot could not overhaul Ferguson before he would reach Ninety Six. They then began to count the number of horsemen that they could raise. Beginning with those under Col. Graham and those of Major Chronicle, Graham's men 160, Chronicle's 20, were to count 200 instead of 180. Campbell mentioned to Chronicle that the lad whom he had with him should not hear their enumeration. Chronicle replied that he was a son of "Old Rugged and Tough;" that his cheek was too well hooped to leak—the lad [Robert Henry] then [listening] is now our surveyor. They numbered on, and found their true number to be between six and seven hundred; but told the soldiers it was between 1100 and 2000 [1200] counting Williams' men.

Orders were then given for all who were unable, from any cause that would hinder him in a severe march, should fall back into the foot troops and give their horses to footmen [who needed them, in order to be properly equipped for the march]; a number of exchanges were made. Further orders were given at Gilbert Town to kill some beeves, which was done; and orders were given for the horse men to be ready to march at a given time, which was very short. Some of the troops who were tardy got none [of the beef?]. The line of march was taken to cross Broad River at Pear's Ford, below the mouth of Green River, to take a near cut on Ferguson on his way to Ninety Six. The day and night were occassionally showery. We marched on, crossing Ferguson's trail in the track (?), and proceeded to the Cowpens and came to a Tory's house, pulled him out of bed, treated him roughly, and asked him at what time Ferguson had passed that place. He said he had not passed at all; that he had torch pine—that we might light it and search, and if we could find the track of an army we might hang him, or do what we pleased with him; and if no sign of an army could be found, he would expect more mild treatment. Search was made and no sign of an army found.

We then camped, and began to send persons to find Ferguson's track. Chronicle proposed to send Enoch Gilmer as one; it was objected to because he was not acquainted with the country. Chronicle said that he could find out any thing better than those acquainted, for he could act any character that he pleased; that he could cry and laugh in the same breath, and those best acquainted would believe that he was in earnest in both; that he could act the fool so that those best acquainted with him would believe him to be deranged; that he was a shrewd, cunning fellow, and a stranger to fear. Hence he was [sent] among others. He went to a Tory's house on Ferguson's trail and stated to him that he had been waiting on Ferguson's way from Twitty's Ford to Ninety-Six, but missed finding him; that he wished to join the army. The Tory replied, that after Ferguson had crossed the river at Twitty's Ford, he had received an express from

Lord Cornwallis for him to join the main army at Charlotte; that he had called in Tarleton, and would call in
his out-posts, and give Gates another defeat, and reduce
North Carolina to British rule as he had South Carolina
and Georgia, and would enter Virginia with a larger
army than ever had been in America. Gilmer gave this
account to the officers. This was some time in the day.
They then commenced marching to the Cherokee Ford
on Broad River. Night came on, and our pilots missed
their way, the night being dark and occasionally raining,
so that when we came near to the river it was near day-
light; and when we came to the river hills it was agreed
that we would send Enoch Gilmer to see whether Ferguson had not been apprised of us and would attack us in
the river. Orders were given to keep our guns dry, for
it was raining. Gilmer was gone for some time, when
his voice was heard in the hollow singing Barney–Linn,
a favorite black-guard song. This was notice that all
was right. Orders were given that the largest horses
should be on the upper side. The order was not obeyed.
The river was deep, but it was remarked that not one was
ducked. After passing the river, it was agreed that
Enoch Gilmer should go ahead, and make all the dis-
coveries about Ferguson that he could. He went off in
a gallop. The officers kept in front of the privates at a
very slow gait—the men cursing and stating if we were
to have a battle, to let it be over, &c.

All were very hungry, and when we would come to a
cornfield, it was soon pulled. The soldiers would cut
part of the raw corn off the cobb, and haul the remainder
to their horses. After travelling some miles, the officers
saw Gilmer's horse at a gate about three-quarters of a
mile ahead. They gave whip to their horses, and went
at full speed to the gate—alighted, and went into the
house. Gilmer was sitting at a table eating. Campbell

exclaimed, "We have got you—you d——d rascal."
Gilmer replied, "a true King's man by G——d." Campbell in order to try Gilmer's metamorphosis, had provided
himself with a rope, with a running noose on it, threw it
over Gilmer's neck. Gilmer commenced crying and begging. Campbell swore that they would hang him on the
bow of the gate—when Chronicle stated that it was
wrong to hang him there, for his ghost would haunt the
women, who were now in tears. Campbell observed that
was right, that we will hang him on the first stooping
limb of a tree that they should pass on the road—then
sending Gilmer along one or two hundred yards, Gilmer
crying and begging for his life, the rope was taken from
his neck, and he mounted his horse, and was asked
what news he had obtained. He stated as follows:—
That when he came to the Tory's house, he professed to
be a true King's man, that he was wishing to join Col.
Ferguson, and desired to know where he was, and that
he had kissed the two Tory women; that the youngest
of the two informed him, that she had been in Ferguson's
camp that morning; that the camp was about three miles
distant from that place; that she had carried him some
chickens; that he was camped on a ridge between two
branches where some deer hunters had a camp the last
Fall. Major Chronicle and Capt. Mattocks stated that
the camp referred to was their camp, and that they well
knew the ground Ferguson was camped on.

Whereupon it was agreed on that they should plan the
battle, as they knew the ground. They rode a short distance by themselves, and reported that it was an excellent place to surround Ferguson's army, as the shooting would all be up hill—that there would be no danger
of our destroying each other; but doubted whether we
had men enough to surround them. It was then instantly
agreed on by all the officers, that we would attempt to

surround our foes. They immediately began to arrange their men, without stopping and assigning to each officer the part he was to take in surrounding the hill. By the time this was done, we were close to our enemy. The last whose duty was to be prescribed was Col. Wm. Graham with his men, who desired leave of absence, alleging that he had received certain intelligence that his wife was dying with the colic, about sixteen miles off, near Armstrong's Ford on the South Fork. Campbell stated to him that should be the greatest inducement for him to stay, that he could carry the news—and if we were successful, it would be to her as good as a dose of medicine. Graham exclaimed, "Oh my dear, dear wife! Must I never see her again?" Campbell in an angry tone of voice turned to Major Chronicle, and said "shall Col. Graham have leave of absence?" To which Chronicle replied—"it is woman's business, let him go." Campbell told Graham he might go. Graham said he must have an escort—Chronicle told him he might have one; Graham chose David Dickey. Dickey said that he would rather be shot in [battle] than go. Chronicle said —"Dave—You must go." Dickey said he would rather be shot on the spot; 'but if I must go, I must go, I must." Then Col. Graham and Dickey immediately took to the woods, and disappeared.*

Campbell then mentioned to Chronicle that as Graham has gone, you must take his place: Turning to Col. Hambright, Campbell asked "have you any objections?" He replied, that it was his wish, as Chronicle best knew the ground. Whereupon Chronicle called "come on, my South Fork boys," and took the lead.

*Col. William Graham must not be confounded with Major (afterwards General) Joseph Graham. They were not related to each other—Col. Graham came from Augusta County, Virginia and settled on the First Broad river then Tryon now Cleveland County. He married Susan, daughter of William Twitty. Previous to this battle he had been a good soldier and Indian fighter and was a popular man. See an honorable sketch of him in "Hunters's Sketches of North Carolna," p. 522.

The hill was surrounded in a few minntes, and the battle commenced. Our enemies had two to our one; of course their fire was double that of ours. We killed 247 of them, and they killed 143 of our side, agreeably to the account of E. Gilmer and Joseph Beatty, supposed to be the most accurate of any. So that they having choice of ground, we fought them two to one; we killed as many more of them as they killed of us, and took more prisoners than we had men to guard them. But we had not a coward to face the hill that day—they all faded off, until within ten minutes of the battle, the last coward left us. Our equals were scarce, and our superiors hard to find. This is the most particular and accurate account, my friend, that I can give you.

Whereupon at the head of the Round-About, I made a similar statement to our chain-bearers, pack-horsemen, &c. Mussentine Matthews made the following reply: "Ah! you would have been a formidable and destructive set of blue hen's chickens among eggs, if each one of you had been provided with a good stick. When anybody pretends to tell the story of that transaction, it would be to his credit to play the game of shut mouth."* This elicited the following reply from Gen. Joseph McDowell:

Before that battle (referring to Ferguson's defeat,) we had sustained two shameful and disastrous defeats—that of Gates by treachery; and that of Sumter by carelessness, in quick succession one after the other—upon which, the Tories flocked to the British camps, and increased their numbers to two or three fold; that the country was over-run, and fairly deluged with them, so much that from the pressure of their numbers, the souls of the brave, from necessity were obliged to cower under its weight,

---

*All we know about Mussentine Matthews is that he represented Iredell County in the House of Commons from 1789 to 1802 continuously. He was either a Tory or a cynic, it seems.

and none but the bravest of the brave withstood the shock.

At the time when the news of Gates' defeat reached Col. Charles McDowell, he had detached Cols. Shelby and Sevier to go round Ferguson's camp to dislodge some British and Tories on the Ennoree, near to Ninety-Six. He then sent an express to Shelby to take care of himself, for Gates was defeated. Whereupon Shelby made the best of his way round Ferguson, and fell in with Charles McDowell and the main body, retreating towards Gilbert Town. Then it was suggested by Shelby, that a sufficient force could be raised over the Mountains, with the assistance from Wilkes and Surry counties, to defeat Ferguson. This was agreed to by all the officers present. The troops were raised without Government orders; each man had to furnish his own provisions, arms, ammunition, horse, and all his equipage, without the value of a gun flint from the public; without pay, or expectation of pay or reward, even to the amount of a Continental dollar depreciated to eight hundred to one. They were all volunteers; they were under no compulsion to go, but each man in advance consulted his own courage, well knowing he was going to fight before his return. They started in a rainy, inclement season of the year, without baggage wagon, pack-horse, or tent cloth, across the most rugged bar of mountains in the State, and almost pathless, having only a hunter's trail to travel, followed Ferguson through all his windings; at length over took him at King's Mountain, where he boasted the morning of the battle, that "he was on King's Mountain, and that he was king of that Mountain, and that God Almighty could not drive him from it." There we overhauled him, fought him two to one—hence their fire was double that of ours; yet we killed 287 [247] of them, to 143 they killed of us. Yet the fate of nations and of battles turn on a pivot. Ferguson, a prudent officer, finding himself beset and surrounded on all sides, ordered his regulars, who had muskets and bayonets, to charge bayonets on Major Chronicle's South Fork boys: The regulars having discharged their muskets at a short distance with effect, in turn the Fork Boys discharged their rifles with fatal effect, and retreated, keeping before the points of the bayonets about twenty feet, until they loaded again, when they discharged their rifles, each man dropping his man. This was treatment that British courage could not stand; they in turn retreated with precipitation; then the flag was hoisted, and all was over.

If they had succeeded in the charge, it would have made a pass-way for his army, and they might have turned on our line on the one side of the hill, and defeated us in detail, or have made good their march to Lord Cornwallis at Charlotte, either of which would have been disastrous to the American cause. We had neither a coward or a traitor to face the hill that day. We were the bravest of the brave; we were a formidable flock of blue hen's chickens of the game blood, of indomitable courage, and strangers to fear. We were well provided with sticks; we made the egg shells—British and Tory skulls—fly, like onion pealings in a windy day; the blue cocks flapped their wings and crowed—"we are all for Liberty these times;" and all was over; our equals were scarce, and our superiors hard to find.

Taking the whole campaign, including the battle, I know of no parallel to it in the annals of ancient or Modern warfare; the nearest was that of the Grecian Leonidas and his army at the battle of Thermopyle with the Geat Xerxes. Leonidas and his army were found, victualled and clothed at public expense; each individual of our army had to find at his own expense; Leonidas' army were under Governmental orders; we were under

no government at all, but were volunteers; Leonidas'
army were furnished with arms and camp equipage: We
had to find our own arms, ammunition and horses at our
own expense; Leonidas' army were uuder Government
pay; we were under no pay or reward, or the expectation
of any; Leonidas' army had choice of ground at the pass
at Thermopyle; our enemies had the boasted choice of
ground; Leonidas' army had to fight superior numbers—
so had we; Leonidas had never a coward—neither had
we any; but Leonidas had a traitor who was his over-
throw and destruction of all but one man: We had
neither coward or traitor to face our enemy—hence we
were successful: Leonidas would have been successful,
and have defeated or put to flight the great Xerxes
if he had not had a traitor aboard; Leonidas' defeat
was the destruction of the fine country of Greece,
and the burning and destruction of their fine city of
Athens, the labor of ages: Our success was the sal-
vation of our country and our liberty. There is no
parallel here: We will see if there is any in modern
times.

The generosity and patriotism of the great Washington has been justly boasted of; he did not charge the
United States anything for his services during the Revolution; he was found his food and camp equipage by the
public, and every thing else that he stood in need of;
his necessary incidental expenses he kept an accurate account of, and they were paid by the public; he was paid
for every thing else but his military services. This has
been justly considered as great generosity and patriotism,
and ought never to be forgotten. But this fight of the
blue hen's chickens threw this into the shade of an
eclipse.

Now we will make the comparison. Washington was
rich, and had no family to provide for; we were poor,

and had families to provide for; he was provided with a horse, victuals, clothing, arms, camp equipage and necessary attendance. We had to provide our own horse, victuals, clothing, arms, ammuition and blankets at our own expense. He charged nothing for his military services; neither did we charge any thing for military services, nor did we receive anything for them; he fought the battles of our country with success; we did the same. The expedition against Ferguson, including the battle at King's Mountain, did not cost the State, or the United States, the worth of a single Continental dollar depreciated down to eight hundred to one. It was all done at the expense of bravery of the actors in that transaction. There is no parallel here.

We will now take a view of the situation of the country after the defeats of Gates and Sumter, and before Ferguson's defeat. Cornwallis was in Charlotte with a large army; Rawdon was in Camden with another large army; Leslie was at Winnsborough with a considerable army; Cruger at Ninety-Six with a large army; McGirt, Cunningham and Brown, each having considerable force, carrying on a savage war-fare of murdering, robbing, burning and destroying. George Lumpkin, Ben. Moore and others in Lincoln county, the chief of plunderers. Tarleton & Wemyss having large bodies of dragoons, the best mounted of any that were ever in the United States. For on the fall of Charleston, the British deluged the country with Counterfeit Continental bills, sending emmisaries through the three Southern States to purchase up all the best horses belonging to the Whigs, at any price. Beside these armies, numerous squads of Tories, whenever they could collect ten or twelve, were plundering, robbing, and destroying the last piece of whig property they could lay their hands on belonging to the whigs. To finish the list, Ferguson with about

ɪ,200 men, three fourths Tories, whose principal business
it was to destroy whig stock: It is to be observed, that
more than one half of their armies consisted of Tories.

This is a statement of facts that needs no proof;
they cannot be contradicted or denied, for every body
knows them to be true. This statement does not take
into view the garrisons at Charleston, Savannah, Augusta
and other places in the lower country, or the numerous
bodies of Tories in the lower part of North Carolina,
South Carolina and Georgia completely under British
rule, and North Carolina at the eve of it. We had no
army in any of the three Southern States, under Governmental orders, of any account that I know of except the
poor fragments of Gates' defeated army, lying near the
Virginia line. Marion's troops were volunteers, for the
State was under British rule. The Mecklenburg Hornets
were volunteers from the counties of Rowan, Lincoln and
Mecklenburg.

From this State of things, Cornwallis could easily have
carried out his avowed purpose of again defeating Gates,
and entering Virginia, with the most numerous army that
had been on the Continent, by calling in some of his
needless out-posts, and these numerous squads of petty-
larceny plunderers, who were raised from poverty to af-
fluence in a few days plundering, and having still the
expectation of further advancement by getting the whig
plantations if he had succeeded—the patriotic State of
Virginia would have had to contend with him and his
army almost single handed, for it could have received
little aid from the conquered States, and but little from
Washington, or the Northern States, as they had their
hands full with Clinton and his New York Tories. This
was the most disastrous period for Liberty and Independence from the time of its Declaration to the end of the
war. Liberty and Independence were then shrouded in

Egyptian darkness. Ferguson's defeat was the turning point in American affairs. The battle, extraordinary as it was, was not more extraordinary than its effects were.

Cornwallis on hearing that Ferguson was defeated, immediately dropped the notion of again defeating Gates and entering Virginia with a numerous army, being already galled by the Mecklenburg Hornets, was panic-struck to think that he would, alas! have, at the same time, to encounter the gaffs and spurs of the blue hens' chickens as soon as he could filch a few days provisions from under the wings of the Hornets, took night's leave of the Hornets' Nest, lest he should disturb the wasps, made a precipitate retrograde march, stopping neither night nor day until he joined Leslie of Winnsborough.

Instantly after Ferguson's defeat, McGirt, Cunningham and Brown quit their robbing, murdering, burning and destroying, and played the game of "the least in sight," and "shut-mouth" into the bargain. Lumpkin, Moore, etc., fled to Nocachey; the petty larceny squads of Tories began to seek their hiding places and holes, like rats and mice when the cat would make her appearance. When Generals Greene and Morgan came from the North with all the force that could be spared from that quarter, with the fragments of Gates' defeated army, the brave and cautious Gen. Morgan found that he was unable to fight Tarleton, fled before him, until Williams' troops, being chiefly South Carolina and Georgia refugees, who fought under Williams at Ferguson's defeat, and the other troops who lived on the east side of the mountains, who fought at the same place, heard of Morgan's retreating before Tarleton, and rushed to his assistance. Being thus reinforced, Gen. Morgan turned about and defeated Tarleton at the Cowpens; Gen. Greene had to retreat before Lord Cornwallis until reinforced by the Mecklenburg Hornets, composed of volunteers from Rowan, Lincoln and Mecklenburg counties. Greene turned upon Cornwallis, and at Guilford made an equal fight, neither having the victory. How would it have been with Generals Greene and Morgan if Ferguson had not been defeated? Tarleton's force would have been greatly increased, and Cornwallis' army would have been more than double the number that appeared on the field of battle at Guilford. All then that Morgan and Greene could have done would have been to retreat and keep out of their way, and permit Cornwallis, agreeably to his avowed intention, to have entered Virginia with the most numerous army that had been in the field since the commencement of the war. Virginia would then have had to contend single-handed with that formidable force, with the assistance of Gen. Greene.

In short, Ferguson's defeat was the turning point in American affairs. The loss of this battle would, in all probability, have been the loss of American Independence and the liberty we now enjoy. I never on any occasion feel such dignified pride as when I think that my name counts one of the number that faced the hill at King's Mountain the day of that battle. Others may think and speak disrespectfully of that transaction who are in favor of monarchy and individual oppression; but that is not Joseph McDowell, nor you, my friend Bob.

I have written down my narrative, and Gen. McDowell's reply to Musentine Matthews which he delivered to the boys at head of the Round-About, on the Stone Mountain, as nearly as memory would serve—thinking that reading it might fiill up a blank in your leisure hours, reflecting on the situation of the times to which the recited facts refer.

Your Friend,

D. VANCE.

ROBERT HENRY'S ACCOUNT.

I will now relate a few facts relative to the battle at King's Mountain that came within my own view, and not related by Col. Vance. In Vance's narrative, he refers to Col. W. Graham's and David Dickey's leaving the army to visit his wife, and Major Billy Chronicle taking his place, and calling on his South Fork boys to follow him. At that time Enoch Gilmer called on Hugh Ewin, Adam Barry and myself to follow him close to the foot of the hill. We marched with a quick step, letting Major Chronicle advance about ten steps before us, but further from the hill than we were, until we met the wing from the other side of the hill, then Chronicle having a military hat, but had let it down to shelter the rain from him, and had it not set up, clapped his hand to it in front, and raised it up, and cried " Face to the hill." The words were scarcely uttered, when a ball struck him and he dropped; and in a second after a ball struck Wm. Rabb, about six feet from Chronicle,* and he dropped. We then advanced up the hill close to the Tory lines: There was a log across a hollow that I took my stand by; and stepping one step back, I was safe from the British fire. I there remained firing until the British charged bayonets. When they made the charge, they first fired their guns, at which fire it is supposed they killed Capt. Mattocks, and J. Boyd, wounded Wm. Gilmer and John Chittim. The Fork boys fired and did considerable execution. I was preparing to fire when one of the British advancing, I stepped [back] and was in the act of cocking my gun when his bayonet was running along the

---

*There is an interesting sketch of Major William Chronicle in " Hunter's Sketches of North Carolina." He lived in the S. E. part of Lincoln, now Gaston county, was born in 1755: his mother first married a McKee, and lived near Armstrong's ford: When McKee died she married a Chronicle, by whom she had Major William Chronicle. Perhaps Col. Graham would have shared Chronicle's fate, at the hand of the sharpshooters if he had remained.

barrel of my gun, and gave me a thrust through my hand and into my thigh; my antagonist and myself both fell. The Fork boys retreated and loaded their guns. I was then lying under the smoke, and it appeared that some of them were not more than a gun's length in front of the bayonets, and the farthest could not have been more than twenty feet in front when they discharged their rifles. It was said that every one dropped his man. The British then retreated in great haste, and were pursued by the Fork boys.

Wm. Caldwell saw my condition, and pulled the bayonet out of my thigh, but it hung to my hand; he gave my hand a kick, and went on. The thrust gave me much pain, but the pulling of it [out] was much more severe. With my well hand I picked up my gun, and found her discharged. I suppose that when the soldier made the thrust, I gripped the trigger and discharged her—the load must have passed through his bladder and cut a main artery of his back, as he bled profusely.

Immediately after Wm. Caldwell drew the bayonet from me, then the word was that the flag was up—the whigs then shouted " Hurra for Liberty," three times at the top of their voices. It was immediately announced that Ferguson was killed. I had a desire to see him, and went and found him dead; he was shot in the face, and in the breast. It was said he had received other wounds. Samuel Talbot turned him over, and got his pocket pistol.

Being in much pain and drouthy, went down, left my gun, being unable to carry her, and when I got near to the branch met David Dickey and Col. Wm. Graham riding his large black horse, wielding his sword round his head, crying at the top of his voice, "Dam the Tories," and ascended the hill. Having seen him get leave of absence at the commencement of the battle to see his wife, I was filled with excitement and a conflict of passion and extreme pain; but this brought on another set of feelings, that may be understood, but I am not possessed of language to describe.

I then went into the branch, drank, bathed my thigh and hand—then went to see whether Major Chronicle and Wm. Rabb were dead or wounded—found them dead. I saw some of the boys hauling Capt. Mattocks and John Boyd down the hill ; and Samuel Martin carrying Wm. Gilmer, who was wounded in the thigh.

Several of the South Fork boys were desirous to start for home that night, and were desirous to know how many were killed on each side. Joseph Beatty and Enoch Gilmer were appointed for that purpose of counting: They reported that 248 British and Tories were killed. and that 143 whigs were killed; they gave no account of the wounded.

In the mean time Hugh Ewin, Andrew Barry and Nathaniel Cook brought their horses and mine; put me on my horse, but could not take my gun. We rode over the battle-ground; saw in some places the dead lay thick, and other places thin. We went about five miles from the battle-ground, and staid for the night. My wounds pained me extremely. Sunday morning we started for home. When we came to the South Fork, the waters were high, and my company would not suffer me to ride the river, but took me across in a canoe, and hauled me home in a slide.

I continued in extreme pain when my mother made a poultice of wet ashes, and applied it to my wounds. This gave me the first ease, On Monday morning by sun-rise Hugh Ewin and Andrew Barry came to see me, and immediately after came several Neutralists, as they called themselves, but were really Tories, to hear the news about the battle, when the following dialogue took place between Ewin and Barry on one part, and the Tories on the other: Is it certain that Col. Ferguson is killed, and his army defeated and taken prisoners?

E. and B. It is certain, for we saw Ferguson after he was dead, and his army prisoners.

Tory. How many men had Col. Ferguson?

E. and B. Nearly 1200, but not quite 1200.

Tory. Where did they get men enough to defeat him?

E. and B. They had the South Carolina and Georgia Refugees, Col. Graham's men, some from Virginia, some from the head of the Yadkin, some from the head of the Catawba, some from over the mountains, and some from every where else.

Tory. Tell us how it happened, and all about it.

E. and B. We met at Gilbert Town, and found that the foot troops could not overtake Ferguson, and we took between six and seven hundred horsemen, having as many or more footmen to follow; and we overtook Ferguson at King's Mountain, where we surrounded and defeated him.

Tory. Ah! That won't do. Between six and seven hundred to surround nearly 1200. It would take more than 2000 to surround and take Col. Ferguson.

E. and B. But we were all of us blue hen's chickens.

Tory. There must have been of your foot and horse in all over 4000. We see what you are about—that is, to catch Lord Cornwallis napping.

Thus ended the dialogue, not more than two hours after sun-rise on Monday; and the Neutralists or Tories immediately departed. It was reported that they immediately swam a horse across the Catawba river by the side of a canoe (the Catawba was much higher than the South Fork,) and gave Lord Cornwallis the news of Ferguson's defeat.

Before my wounds were well, I went to Charlotte, and after Cornwallis had left it, where I met a David Knox, a brother or near relation of James Knox, the grand father of President Polk, who gave me the following information, to wit: That on Monday next after Ferguson's defeat, he, Knox, being a prisoner in the street in Charlotte, that an officer came to the officer of the guard, and the following dialogue took place.

The first officer said to the officer of the guard, Did you hear the news?

Officer of Guard. No, what news?

First Officer. Col. Ferguson is killed, and his whole army defeated and taken prisoners.

Officer of Guard. How can that be—where did the men come from to do that?

First Officer. Some of them were from South Carolina and Georgia Refugees, some from Virginia, some from the head of the Yadkin, some from the head of Catawba, some from over the Mountains, and some from every where else: They met at Gilbert Town, about 2000 desperadoes on horseback, calling themselves blue hen's chickens—started in pursuit of Ferguson, leaving as many footmen to follow. They overtook Col. Ferguson at a place called King's Mountain; there they killed Col. Ferguson after surrounding his army, defeated them and took them prisoners.

Officer of Guard. Can this be true?

First Officer. As true as the gospel, and we may look out for breakers.

Officer of Guard. God bless us!

Whereupon David Knox jumped on a pile of fire-wood in the street, slapped his hands and thighs, and crowed like a cock, exclaiming "Day is at hand!" Hence he was called Peter's Cock, having some analogy to the crowing of the cock when Peter denied his Lord the third time.

It was generally considered about Charlotte and elsewhere, that this exaggerated account, given by the Neutralists, of Col. Campbell's army, foot and horse, at 4000, which carried a strong air of plausibility with it, was the reason why Lord Cornwallis immediately left Charlotte in the night, after the waters were passable, and did not stop day nor night until he met Gen. Leslie at or near Winnsborough.

———

MEM.—Carefully transcribed from the original Manuscript in Robert Henry's hand-writing, sent me by mail for the purpose, by Dr. J. F. E. Hardy, of Asheville, N. C., Jan. 26th, 27th, 28th and early the 29th, 1874.

L. C. DRAPER.

DAVID VANCE.

When the war between the States began, there still lived in North Carolina men and women who had come down to us from Revolutionary times. They were the repositories of many interesting anecdotes and reminiscences of that stirring period. In addition, a mass of documentary matter had been collected by Hawks, Wheeler, Swain, Graham and others ready for the pen of the historian. But the dreadful "clash of resounding arms" in 1861, and the equally momentous events which followed the close of military hostilities suspended completely all efforts in this direction and the minds of men were absorbed in the great political and social questions of the times which involved the very existence of the community.

With returning peace and prosperity loyal hearts and loving hands resumed the work of historical research, but alas! much precious time and valuable matter had been irretrievably lost. The survivors of the patriots of 1776-'81 had passed away and in their graves had been buried the treasures of their recollections; and many valuable papers collected with much care had been destroyed. Yet much has been done and much remains to be done. We can "gather up the fragments" and preserve them for those who may come after us. Incidents, trifling in themselves apparently, but which exhibit the manners of the times and illustrate the character of the men who took part in the establishmant of our government, now become of great interest. In addition there is the obligation—"a pleasing burden"—we bear to preserve the memory and perpetuate the virtues of those brave and good men to whose suffering and wisdom we are in- debted for the blessings we enjoy.

The following sketch of one who took an active part in

the early history of western North Carolina has been prepared chiefly for the use of his descendants. It has been
decided to print it in order that if it shall contain anything of general interest it will be the more easily preserved.

David Vance was descended from that remarkable people, known as Scotch-Irish, who were among the earliest
settlers of the Southern colonies, and from the beginning
exercised a powerful influence in every department of affairs. His father, Samuel, about the middle of the
eighteenth century, lived in Frederick county, Virginia,
near "Zane's Iron Works." His wife was Miss Colville,
and of this marriage there were five sons and three daughters; David, the eldest, having been born about the year
1745. His father removed to south-western Virginia and
settled near Abingdon in 1776, where some of his descendants still reside. At what period David came to
North Carolina is not precisely known, but about the
year 1775 he married, in what is now Burke, but was then
Rowan county, Priscilla Brank; and here, pursuing his
avocation of surveyor and school-teacher, the beginning
of the Revolutionary war found him. He seems to have
been among the first in North Carolina who took up arms
in support of the cause of the Colonies. He was com-
missioned Ensign in the Second North Carolina Continental Regiment on the 8th of June, 1776, and in April
following was promoted to a Lieutenancy. He served
with his regiment until May or June 1778 when, because
of decimation from losses in battle and from sickness the
regiments composing the North Carolina Brigade were
consolidated by act of the Provincial Congress, he, with
many other officers, according to Col. John Patton's return of September 9th, 1778, was sent to Carolina to be
assigned to one of the four regiments which were to be
thereafter organized in North Carolina. He was with his

regiment at Brandywine, Germantown, Monmouth, and during that dreadful winter of 1777-'78 at Valley Forge, and doubtless took part in all the other minor engagements of those campaigns. One of his daughters used to tell his grand-children that, during the privations of the winter at Valley Forge, the officers endeavored to keep up the spirits of their men by promoting games, contests and other amusements, and her father brought home from the war a " Spanish Milled dollar" which had been presented to him by Washington as the prize won in a running match.

It does not seem that he ever re-entered the regular service, but resided with his family on the Catawba river, near Morganton, during the year 1778 and 1779, teaching school. He was the neighbor and fast friend of Charles and Joseph McDowell. When the seat of war was transferred from the Northern to the Southern Colonies and the campaigns of 1780-'81 opened in the Carolinas, he again became an active participant in the field, serving under Generals Rutherford, Davidson and Morgan in the militia and other temporary forces raised from time to time to meet the emergencies resulting from Cornwallis' invasion. He fought at Ramseur's Mill, Musgrove's Mill, Cowpens (probably), and on that glorious day at King's Mountain, where the long struggle for independence and the destiny of a continent were decided. In his narrative of the events connected with that battle he says he "was a captain." It is presumable therefore that in the forces hastily gathered for the purpose of resisting the advance of the British, he commanded a company, most probably in the batallion under Major Joseph McDowell.

The war having been ended and the independence of his country secured, he resumed his peaceful pursuits, taking, however, his share of the burden and responsibility in the grave task of establishing a form of government suitable to the condition and wants of the people. It is impossible for us now to appreciate the gravity of the situation which presented itself to the men of those times. The imperfect records which have been preserved of the discussions of the problems they were called upon to solve disclose the anxieties and difficulties which surrounded them. Much as we admire their bravery, endurance and skill in war, it was in the border-fields of politics and statesmanship their wisdom and patriotism were more fully displayed. When we reflect upon the result of their labors and recall the prosperity and happiness the whole country so long enjoyed in consequence, we are almost impelled to believe the marvellous sagacity they exhibited was of divine inspiration.

Captain Vance, as he was then called, represented Burke county in the General Assembly of 1785-'86 and in 1791. He was one of the commissioners appointed by the legislature of 1785 to carry into effect the act passed at that session for the relief of the "officers, soldiers and seamen who had been disabled in the service of the United States" in the late war, and to adjust the controversies arising from the entries of public lands in " the District of Morgan."

Soon after the treaty of peace with Great Britain, hostilities with the Cherokee Indians, who then occupied that portion the State west of the Blue Ridge, ceased, and the fertile lands of the French Broad Valley began to attract the attention of the emigrant. Some time between the years of 1785 and 1790, Captain Vance crossed the mountains with his family and settled at the head of the lovely little valley of Reems Creek. He here acquired a large and valuable body of land upon which he built a comfortable home—yet standing, a good type of the substantial frontier architecture—in which he reared his family and resided the balance of his life.

This territory was in then Burke county. At the session of the General Assembly of 1791, Captain Vance introduced and had passed the bill creating the county of Buncombe. As this is the genesis of that now famous county, it will not be inappropriate to insert here an extract from the Journal of the House of Commons for Saturday, December 17th, 1791, the General Assembly then sitting at New Berne:

"Mr. Vance presented the petition of the inhabitants of that part of Burke county lying west of the Appalachian Mountain, praying that a part of Rutherford county be made into a separate and distinct county. Mr. William Davidson presented a petition to the same effect; both of which being read, Mr. Vance moved for leave and presented a bill to answer the prayer of the said petitions, which was read the first time, passed and sent to the Senate."

The Journal of the Senate shows that the bill was received and passed by that body on the same day. The Mr. William Davidson referred to in this extract was the representative from Rutherford county, and at that time resided on the south side of the Swannanoa river not far from the present site of the city of Asheville, that part of Buncombe then being, or supposed to be in Rutherford county.

At the organization of the county of Buncombe in April 1792, David Vance was chosen clerk of the County Court, which position he continuously occupied until his death. Some of the records of that court while he was its clerk are extant, and the beauty of his chirography, the order and neatness, as well as the accuracy of his entries, bear witness of his entire qualifications for the duties of his office.

A story is related of him in connection with his office of clerk, which shows something of the manners of the time and the character of the man. On one occasion two young men called at his house, one of whom desired to procure a marriage license. They were invited to enter, and the Captain soon produced from his side-board, a decanter, from which he invited them to refresh themselves. They did so, whereupon the Captain replaced his decanter and proceeded to dispatch the business for which they had come. When they were about to leave, one of the young men ventured to ask for another dram. The old gentleman indignantly refused, and proceeded to read the young man a lecture, which perhaps he never forgot, winding up with the declaration that " such a request had never before been heard of in the house of a gentleman."

About the time he was elected clerk, he was appointed colonel of militia for Buncombe—a position then, and for many years after, regarded as the highest dignity and influence in the county organizations. Thereafter he was known as Colonel Vance.

He, with Gen. Joseph McDowell and Mussendine Matthews were appointed commissioners by act of the General Assembly at the session of 1796 to settle and mark the boundary line between the States of North Carolina and Tennessee. Although the act was passed in 1796 the commissioners did not run the line until the year 1799. They began at White Top Mountain, a point where the boundaries of North Carolina, Virginia and Tennessee meet and ran westwardly, locating the boundary between Tennesse and North Carolina, to a point at the eastern end of the great Smoky Mountains in a gap near where the present Cattalooche turnpike leading from Waynesville to Tennesse, crosses Mt. Starling. This, at that time, was supposed to be the eastern boundary of the Indian Territory.

It was while running this line, the incident occurred which gave rise to the preparation of the accounts of the campaign and Battle of King's Mountain by Colonel

Vance and Robert Henry, Esquire, (the latter being one of the surveyors appointed by the commissioners) known as the " Vance-Henry Narrative."

He survived until the early part of the year 1813, when, having faithfully and honorably accepted and discharged the duties which the conditions of his life demanded; having justly acquired the love and veneration of his fellow-citizens; having lived long enough to see the great principles for which he had fought securely established and his countrymen marching onward toward a glorious and happy future, he peacefully died, leaving behind him the record of a life worthy of the emulation of all men and one which his descendants may proudly contemplate and fondly cherish.

He was buried on a beautiful knoll a short distance north of his residence, a spot selected by himself as a last resting-place, and which, it is said, he often spoke of as "a beautiful place from which to arise on the Resurrection Morn."

He left surviving him, his wife, three sons, Samuel, David and Robert Brank, and five daughters, Jean, who married Hugh Davidson; Elizabeth, who married Mitchell Davidson and after his death Samuel W. Davidson; Sarah, who married —— McLean; Priscilla who married —— Whitson, and Celia, who married Benjamin S. Brittain. Samuel and Jean, Sarah and Priscilla, with their husbands, about the beginning of this century, removed to and settled upon the lands in Tennesse on the Duck river, which their father had provided for them. They left numerous children, some of whom, together with many of their children, still reside in the vicinity. The late Judge Hugh Law Davidson and his brother Robert B. Davidson, who is still living, a highly esteemed citizen and a member of the Bar at Shelbyville, Tennessee, were the sons of Jean.

David lived and died in the county of Buncombe. He was the father of Hon. Zebulon B. Vance and Gen. Robert B. Vance.

Elizabeth and her husband settled on Jonathans creek in Haywood county, where they reared a large family. Hon. Allen T. Davidson, now living in Asheville, is one of their sons.

Robert Brank, never married, suffering from a physical infirmity which forbade a more active life, was carefully educated and became a physician, though he never practiced his profession. He resided in Asheville. While still quite young, he entered public life and was elected to Congress, succeeding Felix Walker, the first representative from the Transmontane District. At the next election he was defeated by Hon. Samuel Carson,, and in November following was killed in a duel with that gentleman—the unhappy event being the result of their canvas.

Celia, the youngest child, with her husband, located in that part of the county of Haywood subsequently included in Macon county; but soon afterwards upon the organization of Cherokee county removed to Murphy, where she died in 1876, leaving a number of children and grandchildren, many of whom reside in that vicinity, useful and respected citizens.

Although the condition of the country denied to Colonel Vance the opportunities for collegiate training, he seems to have had a taste for books. At the time of his death he had accumulated a respectable library for that period. He was careful that his children should enjoy all the educational advantages which were accessible to them.

He was distinguished among his contemporaries for his soundness of judgment, integrity of conduct, firmness of purpose and public spirit.

He accumulated a handsome estate for those times, which he disposed of by will prepared by himself. It is an exceedingly interesting document, and perhaps no better index to his character now remains to us or a more fitting close of this imperfect sketch can be made than that contained in the following extracts from it:

"I hope I may be excused for expatiating in divers parts of this last solemn act upon subjects that require clearness and plainness, for I have heard of so many instances of confusion and disagreement in families, and so much doubt and difficulty for want of absolute clearness in the testaments of departed persons, that I have often concluded (were there no other reasons but those which respect the peace of surviving friends) that the last act in its designation and operation, ought not to be the t in its composition or making; but should be the re- of cool deliberation; and (as is more frequently than aid) of a sound mind and memory, which are sel- to be met with, but with sound health. All pretenses of insanity of mind are likewise prevented when a testator is pointed and clear in what he wills; all cavils about words are obviated; the obliged are assured, and they enjoy the benefit, for whom the benefit was intended.

"I, David Vance, of the county of Buncombe, in the State of North Carolina, being of sound and perfect mind and memory, as I hope these presents, drawn up by myself and written with my own hand, will testify," &c.

In disposing of some old slaves, he directs:

"It is my will and desire that they have full liberty, and I do by these presents give them full liberty, to go and live with any of my children where their own children live, not as slaves, but as old acquaintances, who labored and spent their strength to raise my said children and their own also. I enjoin it upon my children who may have the children of said black old people not to confine them, but to let them go awhile to one, and awhile to another, where their children may be; and I enjoin it upon my children to see that the evenings of the lives of those black people slide down as comfortable as may be. * * * * And I charge and adjure my negroes, old and young, as they will answer to God, to be obedient and obliging to their mistress and not vex or contrary her in old age. * * * *

And now, having disposed of and settled all my worldly business and concerns, do I with a lively faith, humbly lay hold of the meritorious death and sufferings of Christ Jesus and hope and trust thro' His atonement to triumph in redeeming love, the ceaseless age of eternity."

9 783337 182335